YOU KNOW YOU'RE AN OLD FART WHEN...

by
DUSTY RUMSEY

CCC PUBLICATIONS • **LOS ANGELES**

Published by

CCC Publications
21630 Lassen Street
Chatsworth, CA 91311

Manufactured in the United States Of America

Cover © 1993 CCC Publications

Interior illustrations © 1993 CCC Publications

Cover & Interior art by Dusty Rumsey

Interior layout & production by Oasis Graphics

ISBN: 0-918259-52-5

If your local U.S. bookstore is out of stock, copies of this book may be obtained by mailing check or money order for $3.95 per book (plus $2.50 to cover postage and handling) to: CCC Publications; 21630 Lassen St.; Chatsworth, CA 91311.

Pre-publication Edition - 7/93
First Printing - 2/94
Second Printing - 5/94

DEDICATION

Thanks to Barbara for this hilarious idea.

Special thanks to Donna, Chandler, The Parents (older farts than I, but just barely), Mark and Cliff at CCC, and anyone who finds this book funny.

INTRODUCTION

From 30 on, everyone is worried about growing old.

Have you ever uttered one of the following phrases?

"That's not music, that's a bunch of noise!"

"In my day, we did things right or we didn't do them at all!"

"When I was your age we didn't have it so easy!"

Are you guilty of wearing socks and sandals at the beach? Did you cancel your tee time due to prostate surgery? Are you more comfortable in fuzzy slippers than heels? Do you own an RV?

If you answered YES to any of these questions, guess what?

You're an OLD FART!

Congratulations, you've just begun the rite of passage from infancy to senility and what a journey it is! **You Know You're An Old Fart When...** will help you see the light (eyesight permitting) and get ready for the day when people call you an OLD FART!

But don't be too surprised to discover you already are an OLD FART!

YOU KNOW YOU'RE AN
OLD FART WHEN....

YOU HAVE A WINNEBAGO COVERED WITH
TRAVEL STICKERS

YOU KNOW YOU'RE AN OLD FART WHEN....

Forty-seven straight hours of XXX videos, and not so much as a quiver.

ADULT FILMS HAVE NO EFFECT
ON YOUR LIBIDO

YOU KNOW YOU'RE AN OLD FART WHEN....

YOU CAN'T TELL WHO PASSED GAS –
YOU OR YOUR DOG

YOU KNOW YOU'RE AN OLD FART WHEN....

YOU HAVE A RESERVED SEAT
AT A BINGO HALL

YOU KNOW YOU'RE AN OLD FART WHEN....

A BOWEL MOVEMENT IS AN
EVENT WORTH RECORDING

YOU KNOW YOU'RE AN OLD FART WHEN....

An hour had passed since grandpa paused and the children began to get restless.

YOU FORGET THE MORAL OF THE STORY YOU'RE TELLING

YOU KNOW YOU'RE AN OLD FART WHEN....

"Oh, that was good – know any other dog jokes?"

YOU FIND STIMULATING CONVERSATION
IN THE COMPANY OF CATS

YOU KNOW YOU'RE AN OLD FART WHEN....

YOU ACCESSORIZE YOUR WALKER

YOU KNOW YOU'RE AN OLD FART WHEN....

Boris' career as a flasher was greatly hindered by his extremely poor vision.

YOUR EYEGLASSES ARE THICKER THAN YOUR WAISTLINE

YOU KNOW YOU'RE AN OLD FART WHEN....

YOUR ANKLES GROW LARGER
THAN YOUR BREASTS

YOU KNOW YOU'RE AN OLD FART WHEN....

YOUR HEAD DOESN'T CLEAR THE
STEERING WHEEL IN YOUR CAR

YOU KNOW YOU'RE AN OLD FART WHEN....

YOU RARELY LEAVE THE GOLF
CART TO HIT A SHOT

YOU KNOW YOU'RE AN OLD FART WHEN....

Sunshine loved the Earth, but she hated its gravity.

YOUR STATUS AS A LIBERATED WOMAN BECOMES A BIOLOGICAL BURDEN

YOU KNOW YOU'RE AN
OLD FART WHEN....

YOU'RE IN THE BLACK MARKET
FOR COUNTERFEIT HANDICAPPED
PARKING STICKERS

YOU KNOW YOU'RE AN OLD FART WHEN....

In retrospect, the Sports Illustrated swimsuit issue may not have been the ideal birthday gift for Grandpa Hatley.

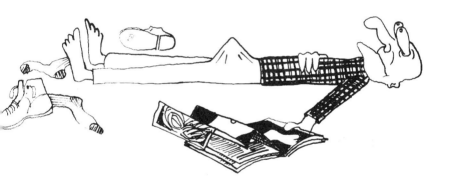

CENTERFOLDS PUT A SERIOUS
STRAIN ON YOUR HEART

YOU KNOW YOU'RE AN OLD FART WHEN....

YOU METICULOUSLY STYLE THE THREE
REMAINING HAIRS ON YOUR HEAD

YOU KNOW YOU'RE AN
OLD FART WHEN....

CHILDREN THINK YOU'RE A
HOLLYWOOD SPECIAL EFFECT

YOU KNOW YOU'RE AN OLD FART WHEN....

YOU GET A PERSONALIZED ROCKING
CHAIR FOR YOUR BIRTHDAY

YOU KNOW YOU'RE AN OLD FART WHEN....

AN ERECTION IS JUST ANOTHER
DISTANT MEMORY

YOU KNOW YOU'RE AN OLD FART WHEN....

Ansel and Agnes
prepare to suck face

YOU REMOVE YOUR TEETH TO FRENCH KISS

YOU KNOW YOU'RE AN OLD FART WHEN....

THE FIRST EIGHT DIGITS OF YOUR
SOCIAL SECURITY NUMBER ARE ZEROS

YOU KNOW YOU'RE AN
OLD FART WHEN....

That clinched it! Lamar had now pinched every nurse in intensive care.

NURSE-PINCHING IS YOUR NUMBER ONE SPORT

YOU KNOW YOU'RE AN OLD FART WHEN....

BIRDS NEST IN YOUR TOUPEE

YOU KNOW YOU'RE AN OLD FART WHEN....

A SHOUTING MATCH REQUIRES
AMPLIFICATION

YOU KNOW YOU'RE AN OLD FART WHEN....

This was it!
The mother lode!

ALL BERMUDA SHORTS **HALF** OFF!

Knee Socks 6 PR 1⁰⁰

YOU GET REALLY PUMPED FOR A SALE ON
BERMUDA SHORTS AND KNEE SOCKS

YOU KNOW YOU'RE AN
OLD FART WHEN....

Sybil was still working some
of the kinks out of her new
hip replacement.

YOUR BODY IS A COLLECTION OF
REPLACEMENT PARTS

YOU KNOW YOU'RE AN OLD FART WHEN....

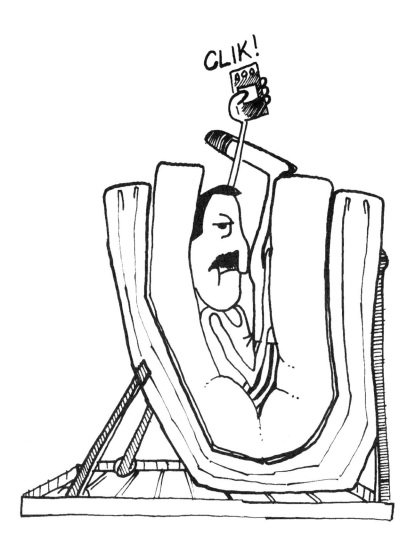

YOU OWN AN ADJUSTABLE BED

YOU KNOW YOU'RE AN OLD FART WHEN....

Uncle Renfield's suggestion for a game of catch had turned into an ugly version of "keep away."

YOU HAVE NEPHEWS WHO
DON'T RESPECT YOU

YOU KNOW YOU'RE AN OLD FART WHEN....

Fresh out of cataract surgery, Willard's new look lands him a spot as front man for the "Hate Mamas."

YOU WEAR SUNGLASSES FOR PROTECTION RATHER THAN STYLE

YOU KNOW YOU'RE AN
OLD FART WHEN....

Parnell fought mightily, but in the end, the younger, stronger, 8-pound bass wound up the victor.

FISHING BECOMES A DANGEROUS
UNDERTAKING

YOU KNOW YOU'RE AN OLD FART WHEN....

YOU HIT THE BEACH WITH A COOLER
FULL OF CHILLY MAALOXES

YOU KNOW YOU'RE AN
OLD FART WHEN....

YOU DISCOVER YOUR REFLEXES
AREN'T WHAT THEY USED TO BE

YOU KNOW YOU'RE AN OLD FART WHEN....

YOUR BODY MAKES THE SAME
SOUNDS AS YOUR CEREAL

YOU KNOW YOU'RE AN OLD FART WHEN....

Aunt Gloria outlines her plans for Cousin Ned in her will.

YOUR RELATIVES SUCK UP TO
YOU WHEN YOU'RE SICK

YOU KNOW YOU'RE AN OLD FART WHEN....

YOU TAKE SHUFFLEBOARD A
LITTLE TOO SERIOUSLY

YOU KNOW YOU'RE AN OLD FART WHEN....

YOU TALK TO INANIMATE OBJECTS

YOU KNOW YOU'RE AN
OLD FART WHEN....

YOUR LIFE REVOLVES AROUND
FIELD TRIPS

YOU KNOW YOU'RE AN OLD FART WHEN....

YOU RESORT TO DRASTIC MEASURES
TO REMOVE WRINKLES

YOU KNOW YOU'RE AN OLD FART WHEN....

The Catskill

Waco Snake Ranch

The Grand Canyon

Graceland

YOU HAVE MORE THAN THREE PHOTOS
OF YOURSELF POSED IN FRONT OF
TOURIST ATTRACTIONS

YOU KNOW YOU'RE AN OLD FART WHEN....

"Yes," Raymond thought, "it just doesn't get any better than this..."

YOU ATTEND YOUR SECOND
METAL DETECTOR TOURNAMENT

YOU KNOW YOU'RE AN
OLD FART WHEN....

Suddenly and without
warning, Herb's ties were
back in fashion.

YOUR TIE COLLECTION GOES IN AND OUT
OF FASHION MORE THAN TWICE

YOU KNOW YOU'RE AN
OLD FART WHEN....

Alvin sat and waited – at any
moment his bowels might move.

THE BIGGEST BUZZ YOU CAN TIE ON
COMES FROM A BOTTLE OF GERITOL

YOU KNOW YOU'RE AN OLD FART WHEN....

When would that dam dog learn? Slippers! They're just slippers!

ARF ARF! ARF ARF!

YOU OWN MORE PAIRS OF FUZZY PINK SLIPPERS THAN HIGH HEELS

YOU KNOW YOU'RE AN
OLD FART WHEN....

YOU ACTUALLY FIND HUMOR IN THE
OLD "PULL MY FINGER" TRICK

YOU KNOW YOU'RE AN OLD FART WHEN....

Normally, Trent could get
out of a space in one try
– if no one was watching.

DRIVING A STICKSHIFT ISN'T AS
MUCH FUN AS IT USED TO BE

YOU KNOW YOU'RE AN OLD FART WHEN....

ALL YOUR FAVORITE SONGS APPEAR
ON A COMPILATION ALBUM

YOU KNOW YOU'RE AN OLD FART WHEN....

YOUR IDEA OF AEROBICS IS CHANGING
THE STATIONS ON THE TV REMOTE

YOU KNOW YOU'RE AN OLD FART WHEN....

YOU HAVE MORE HAIR IN YOUR NOSE
AND EARS THAN ON YOUR HEAD

YOU KNOW YOU'RE AN OLD FART WHEN....

YOU LOOK RIDICULOUS IN
HIGH TOPS

YOU KNOW YOU'RE AN
OLD FART WHEN....

For a fleeting moment,
Irma had a mental
picture of the van grace-
fully arcing into the air
and over a cliff.

YOU STOP BUYING SPORTS CARS

YOU KNOW YOU'RE AN OLD FART WHEN....

YOUR FAVORITE VIDEO GAME
IS STILL "PONG"

YOU KNOW YOU'RE AN OLD FART WHEN....

YOUR KIDS HAVE LAPTOP COMPUTERS
AND YOU STILL USE A TYPEWRITER

YOU KNOW YOU'RE AN
OLD FART WHEN....

"Ah-ah-ah-ah-stayin'
alive, stayin' alive."

YOU ACTUALLY CONSIDER WEARING
ONE OF YOUR OLD LEISURE SUITS

53

YOU KNOW YOU'RE AN
OLD FART WHEN....

YOU CAN'T UNDERSTAND THE LYRICS
TO THIS YEAR'S GRAMMY WINNER

YOU KNOW YOU'RE AN
OLD FART WHEN....

Lookout babes,
here I come!

YOU STROLL THE BEACH SPORTING
SOCKS AND A "GOLFER TAN"

YOU KNOW YOU'RE AN OLD FART WHEN....

PRESIDENTIAL CANDIDATES LOOK
YOUNG TO YOU

YOU KNOW YOU'RE AN
OLD FART WHEN....

YOU CONSTANTLY STRIKE UP CONVERSATIONS
ABOUT THE WEATHER

YOU KNOW YOU'RE AN OLD FART WHEN....

YOUR RECORD COLLECTION DWARFS
YOUR CD COLLECTION

YOU KNOW YOU'RE AN OLD FART WHEN....

YOU NO LONGER DO YOUR
OWN YARDWORK

YOU KNOW YOU'RE AN OLD FART WHEN....

She was thin and clammy, but could she dance!

YOUR ONLY DANCE PARTNER IS
AN IV STAND

YOU KNOW YOU'RE AN OLD FART WHEN....

YOU THINK OF MADONNA FIRST AS A
BIBLICAL CHARACTER, SECOND AS A POP STAR

YOU KNOW YOU'RE AN OLD FART WHEN....

PEOPLE MARVEL AT THE VINTAGE
AUTOS IN YOUR CHILDHOOD PHOTOS

YOU KNOW YOU'RE AN OLD FART WHEN....

A VISIT WITH OLD FRIENDS MEANS
A TRIP TO THE CEMETERY

YOU KNOW YOU'RE AN
OLD FART WHEN....

YOU MAKE THE TRANSITION FROM
JOGGER TO POWER WALKER

YOU KNOW YOU'RE AN OLD FART WHEN....

THE ONLY JUNK MAIL YOU GET
IS FUNERAL PLOT PROMOTIONS

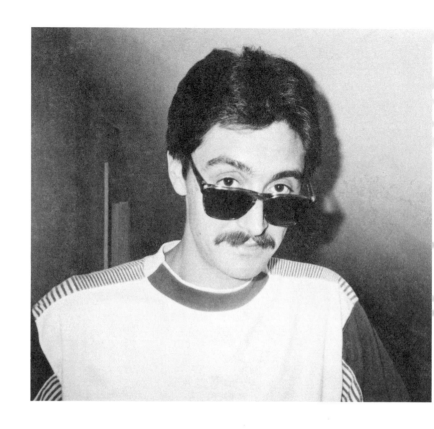

ABOUT THE AUTHOR

Author/Illustrator Rhodes "Dusty" Rumsey resides in Richmond, Virginia, with his wife Donna and daughter Chandler, where he owns and operates Rumsey Productions, a video production company.

In between scripts, shoots and edit sessions, he writes and illustrates humorous books, including "Gifts I Almost Got You" and "UnCivil War."

TITLES BY CCC PUBLICATIONS

NEW PARTY BOOKS   (Available: May 1994)

Retail $4.95
THINGS YOU CAN DO WITH A USELESS MAN
AIR TRAVEL??? I'D RATHER WALK!
MARITAL BLISS & OTHER OXYMORONS
THE VERY VERY SEXY DOT-TO-DOT BOOK
BASTARD'S GUIDE TO BUSINESS SURVIVAL
THE DEFINITIVE FART BOOK
THE TOTAL WIMP'S GUIDE TO SEX
THE CAT OWNER'S SHAPE UP MANUAL
LIFE'S MOST EMBARRASSING MOMENTS

Retail $3.95
PMS CRAZED: TOUCH ME & I'LL KILL YOU!
RETIRED: LET THE GAMES BEGIN
MALE BASHING: WOMEN'S FAVORITE PASTIME
THE OFFICE FROM HELL
FOOD & SEX
BUT OSSIFER, IT'S NOT MY FAULT
YOU KNOW YOU'RE AN OLD FART WHEN...
HOW TO REALLY PARTY!!!
HOW TO SURVIVE A JEWISH MOTHER

1994 NEW TRADE PAPERBACKS   -   Retail $4.95

SHARING THE ROAD WITH IDIOTS   **jan**
GREATEST ANSWERING MACHINE MESSAGES **jan**
1001 REASONS TO PROCRASTINATE   **feb**
FITNESS FANATICS   **mar**
THE WORLD'S GREATEST PUT-DOWN LINES   **apr**
HORMONES FROM HELL II   **may**
YOUNGER MEN ARE BETTER THAN RETIN-A   **jul**
RED HOT MONOGAMY   **[$6.95]   jul**
ROSS PEROT: DON'T QUOTE ME **aug**

(cont.)

BEST SELLING TRADE PAPERBACKS - Retail $4.95

HORMONES FROM HELL   [$5.95]
KILLER BRAS & OTHER HAZARDS OF THE 50'S
BETTER TO BE OVER THE HILL THAN UNDER IT
HUSBANDS FROM HELL
HOW TO ENTERTAIN PEOPLE YOU HATE
THE UGLY TRUTH ABOUT MEN
WHAT DO WE DO NOW??
TALK YOUR WAY OUT OF A TRAFFIC TICKET
THE BOTTOM HALF

BEST SELLING TRADE PAPERBACKS - Retail $3.95

NO HANG-UPS
NO HANG-UPS II
NO HANG-UPS III
GETTING EVEN WITH THE ANSWERING MACHINE
NEVER A DULL CARD
WORK SUCKS!
THE PEOPLE WATCHER'S FIELD GUIDE
THE UNOFFICIAL WOMEN'S DIVORCE GUIDE
YOUR GUIDE TO CORPORATE SURVIVAL
THE ABSOLUTE LAST CHANCE DIET BOOK
FOR MEN ONLY (How To Survive Marriage)
SUPERIOR PERSON'S GUIDE TO IRRITATIONS
GIFTING RIGHT
HOW TO GET EVEN WITH YOUR EXes
HOW TO SUCCEED IN SINGLES BARS
OUTRAGEOUS BUMPER-SNICKERS [$2.95]

ACCESSORIES

THE GUILT BAG [$4.95]
THE "MAGIC BOOKMARK" BOOK COVER [$2.95]

NO HANG-UPS - CASSETTES   - Retail. $4.98)

Vol. I: GENERAL MESSAGES
Vol. II: BUSINESS MESSAGES
Vol. III: 'R' RATED MESSAGES
Vol. IV: SOUND EFFECTS ONLY
Vol. V: CELEBRI-TEASE